The True Diary of Carly Ann Potter

MICHAELA MORGAN

Illustrated by Dee Shulman

OXFORD
UNIVERSITY PRESS

OXFORD
UNIVERSITY PRESS

Great Clarendon Street, Oxford OX2 6DP

Oxford University Press is a department of the University of Oxford.
It furthers the University's objective of excellence in research, scholarship,
and education by publishing worldwide in

Oxford   New York
Auckland   Cape Town   Dar es Salaam   Hong Kong   Karachi
Kuala Lumpur   Madrid   Melbourne   Mexico City   Nairobi
New Delhi   Shanghai   Taipei   Toronto

With offices in
Argentina   Austria   Brazil   Chile   Czech Republic   France   Greece
Guatemala   Hungary   Italy   Japan   Poland   Portugal   Singapore
South Korea   Switzerland   Thailand   Turkey   Ukraine   Vietnam

Oxford is a registered trade mark of Oxford University Press
in the UK and in certain other countries

British Library Cataloguing in Publication Data
Data available

ISBN: 978-0-19-918397-5

11 13 15 17 19 20 18 16 14 12

Available in packs
Stage 13 More Stories B Pack of 6:
ISBN: 978-0-19-918396-8
Stage 13 More Stories B Class Pack:
ISBN: 978-0-19-918403-3
Guided Reading Cards also available:
ISBN: 978-0-19-918405-7

Cover artwork by Dee Shulman
Photograph of Michaela Morgan © Richard Drewe

Printed in Malaysia by
MunSang Printers Sdn Bhd

Paper used in the production of this book is a natural, recyclable product
made from wood grown in sustainable forests. The manufacturing process
conforms to the environmental regulations of the country of origin.

1st January New Year's Day

What about this then?

I've got a brand new five year diary (with a lock!) and a new ink pen. I've decided to write in my new diary *every day* WITHOUT FAIL. CROSS MY HEART.

my mum

the dog

my dad

our baby

ME!!

my brother

The Potter Family

This diary was a present from one of my cousins – Zoe.

'So thoughtful,' says my mum. 'She always was a sweet girl.'

very old photo of Zoe and me. (and dog) Aren't we sweet (YUK!)

I never liked her that much myself but this present is brilliant. She sent one to my brother, Fishface, too – but I bet he'll never write anything in HIS.

I've been dying to write in mine but I've had to wait till today. January 1st. The first day of a NEW YEAR and the first page of a NEW DIARY and a NEW and BETTER me.

I've read some other diaries. Anne Frank*, Zlata*, Adrian Mole* (see notes thoughtfully provided at bottom of page). They are all fantastic records of important times and the children who wrote them became

FIGURES OF HISTORICAL IMPORTANCE

So that's what I'm going to be from now on.

STATUE OF CARLY ANN POTTER AND HER FAMOUS DIARY

* Notes from C.A. Potter for Future Generations.

Anne Frank kept a diary during the Second World War when she was hiding from the enemy. It is very famous and brilliant and sad and important and it is called The Diary of Anne Frank.

Zlata wrote a diary when her home town was bombed and attacked in Bosnia. Her diary was made into a book and read all over the world. It is very famous but a bit long. It is called Zlata's Diary.

Adrian Mole kept a very funny diary (called The Secret Diary of Adrian Mole) but I'm not sure it is altogether TRUE.

Future generations will be able to read my diary (maybe they'll study it in school!). They will say:

Thanks to Carly Ann Potter we have a perfect record of the end of the century. Bless her. She has made history interesting for us.

CARLY ANN POTTER

She was so young and yet so talented. Why, she even thought of making little explaining notes for us.

And her handwriting is — so neat! So beautiful! So artistic. The choice of coloured inks was a masterstroke!

Unfortunately, I haven't got any more space on this page so history will have to wait till tomorrow for more news from Carly Ann Potter, FIGURE of HISTORICAL IMPORTANCE ...

my brother, Fishface. ↑

Real name Christopher Potter. When he was a baby the word Christopher was too hard for him (he's not much brighter now to tell you the truth). He used to say his name was "Fisher," so everyone called him Fisher except me. I call him Fishface. I think you can guess why.

2nd January

Yesterday I decided on my New Year's Resolutions*. I have given them great thought and record them here.

I, *Carly Ann Potter*, hereby make the following resolutions:

I promise to:

1. Write in my diary *every single day*. This is a so~~lem~~ solemn promise to myself and to future generations.

→ good one- think I'll decorate the cover now.

SAVE THE WHALE

---

* Notes for Future Generations.
On the first day of a new year people make promises to themselves to make them better people in the new year. These promises are known as RESOLUTIONS.
They are usually things like:
(For grown-ups) I will stop smoking.
(For ~~sensibel~~ sensible children) I will try to eat fewer chocolates and be a kinder person.
(For brothers like mine) I will try to look less like a stupid fish.

To comb the dog out more often. I will not let him get all tangled and fuzzy so he looks like a four-legged bird's nest, complete with twigs and leaves and such and has to go for expensive clips at the vets.

dog

bird's nest

 To be nicer to my brother. I promise *not* to call my brother a dork, or a nerd, or even Fishface (even though he DOES look like a goldfish when he's chewing gum and his mouth is going open-close, open-close). But this sort of language would not be good for a figure of such historical importance as I am going to be.

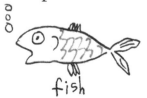

fish

my brother

4. To save money so I can buy ~~sensbul~~ sensible things and not fritter my precious money away on such things as stick-on purple nails which only get stuck in the dog's fur anyway and could take your eye out.

Nail found in the Christmas Pud. Oops! →

5. To improve my WORD POWER, to use long words and look them up in my new ~~diktionry~~ dictionary (with thesaurus) to check on spellings.

The dictionary (with thesaurus) was a present from one of the aunties – well, at least it was better than the orange SPOTTY knickers she sent last year.

 To be a good and valuable human being, kind and generous to my friends, my brother, and all dumb animals.

To use my new Christmas present camera (from another of the many mad aunties) to keep a careful record of my life and times.

It's not easy taking your own photo. That's why I look a bit weird in this one.

Not to eat any more chocolate *ever* but to eat fruit and to have a

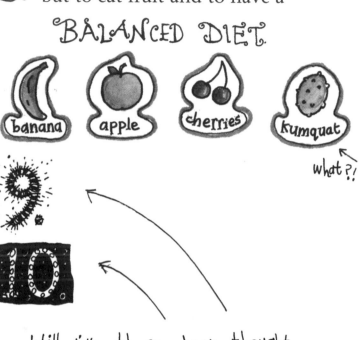

BALANCED DIET.

banana · apple · cherries · kumquat

what?!

Will give these deep thought...

nope-no ideas..

This diary-keeping is ~~ecsausting~~ exhausting (very tiring). I'll have a rest now and go round and see Natalie.

Oops, I missed a few days of the diary. Never mind.

I've told Natalie about my diary and she said I must be sure to tell the future generations all about her. She wants to be a famous historical figure too.

So here is everything you ever wanted to know (and more) about Natalie McNulty:

photo of Natalie McNulty taken by C.A. Potter in my bedroom.

Natalie McNulty

1. Natalie McNulty is the best friend of Carly Ann Potter.

2. She is more like a sister than my real sister is (though my real sister is only about one year old, so it's hard to have a good chat with her).

My baby sister

3. At school they call Natalie and me 'the twins' because we do everything the same. 'Where Natalie leads, Carly follows,' says Miss Sims.

'If Natalie McNulty put her hand in the fire, you would too!' says my mum. (This is COMPLETE NONSENSE. We don't even HAVE a fire.)

Natalie and Carly like 2 Peas in a Pod !! → Pea Pod

4. Some people call Natalie, 'Natalie McNutty' or 'Nuttily the Nutty' and 'Utterly McNutterly'. This is *their* idea of a joke. Natalie is not nutty. True, she does do *some* crazy things sometimes – then Miss Sims says, 'Natalie McNulty, you've got carried away again!'

brazil nut

cashew nut

Natalie Nut Ha Ha!!

5. They call me Carly Potty sometimes or Carly the Potty. I don't think it's all that funny myself. Natalie says not to bother about it. Natalie says famous artists and people of historical importance have often been misunderstood.

It's called a potato – it's good to eat.

HA! HA! HA! HA!

Sir Walter Raleigh – ahead of his time.

6. Natalie has a complete collection of Star Wars videos, books, toys, and even a costume. She is now mad about the **X FILES** *

Natalie in her Star Wars costume

7. Natalie and I are both members of the drama club. We are both BRILLIANT actresses and have decided to be famous film stars or pop stars when we grow up. Though I'd quite like to be a vet, too, or a teacher – maybe an air hostess.

* This is one of the things on TV that I'm not supposed to watch. Mum says it's too scary and... **Aaagh...** It **IS!**

28th January   Chinese New Year

New Year in China! Why now? Do I
have to make even more resolutions?
I shall have to think about this.

All this thinking gives me
a headache. Better stop now.

31st January

I've looked back in my diary to check
on my resolutions. Some of them don't
seem so ~~sensibble~~ sensible now. I've
decided I *should* carry on eating
chocolate after all. This is not *just*
because I'd forgotten my resolution and
eaten quite a bit of chocolate – it's also
out of kindness.

You see, I'd got a selection box from one of my aunties and it would have been ungrateful not to eat it all after my aunty had gone to the trouble of buying it for me. Then there were the Christmas decorations. We had a bumper harvest this year – chocolate reindeer, chocolate santas, chocolate snowmen, chocolate angels. At first I thought I might just nibble an angel wing – or two – then I realized how awful it would be if my Fishface of a brother got to eat my share. What sort of example would that set for future generations?

So fair shares for sisters and GIRL POWER

oops-
a bit of
chocolate
↓ angel

a lot →
of
chocolate
santas!

However, I DO make sure I eat fruit (which is very good for you and ESSENTIAL for a BALANCED DIET) as well. I've just eaten a banana chew *and* a pear drop which must count as fruit.

unhealthy

healthy
(after pear drop)

I will never miss another day of my diary.

I owe it to history.

4th February ←(oops)

Oh, well. I had netball practice one evening. Then a match. On Thursday, Mum made me tidy my room.

Bad mood day

On Friday Natalie came round for tea so I simply didn't have TIME to write in my diary even though I really REALLY wanted to. (I wanted to. I wished to. I desired and LONGED to. I hoped, hankered and YEARNED to. Wow! Word Power or what!!!)

On the plus side I did comb the dog out and she looks very shiny now. (I used my brother's hair gel 'for extra shine and control'.) We dried her with a hairdryer and Natalie put a few of my mum's heated hair rollers in her fur.

Before   After

I don't think the dog likes it much.
She looks a bit embarrassed. She's used
to looking like a small hedge. Mum said
I'd done a very good job but then she
went and ruined it all by saying,

This is a secret diary and I can lock it
tight but I owe it to history to be
completely truthful so I have to say
that, truthfully, my mum NAGS a bit
(quite a lot actually).

5th February

Ha! You see! The very next day and I'm filling my diary in. I am NOT the sort of person who fails to keep a promise.

The trouble is it's Sunday and there's nothing to write about. History will have to record that Sundays at my house were ... boring.

Think I'll go round and see Natalie.

6th February   Waitangi Day, New Zealand

Sadly, nothing happened between Sunday and today.

So there was really no point in doing the diary.

History doesn't want stuff like:

Monday: Nothing happened.

Tuesday: Much the same.

Wednesday: Still nothing.

Thursday: Too bored to write anything.

So I thought it would be best if I just write when I have something to say.

And that's all I have to say today.

Think I'll go round and see Natalie.

10th February

Today we got a letter at our house.

We don't often get letters ('Just bills,' says my dad). This one was more of a note really. I've stuck it in the diary as a HISTORICAL DOCUMENT. Here it is:

8th February

Dear Aunty Maureen, Uncle John, Christopher, Carly and Baby,

How are you all? I am well but do not have a job at the moment. I would like to get a job in London so I wonder if I could stay at your house while I look for one? I would pay rent of course and then I would move out and rent my own flat when I get a job.

My mum said you wouldn't mind me asking if I could move in on the 13th – this Friday. Mum could drive me to your place.

Please phone to say what you decide.

Love Zoe

X

My mum said, 'It would be nice to see Zoe again. She's such a sweet girl.'

My dad said, 'The rent would come in handy.'

Fishface said, 'She could have Carly's room.'

I said, 'NO WAY! NO! NO! DEFINITELY NOT!' So of course she's coming – and I've got to share the baby's room.

It is SO UNFAIR

Death to Zoe

unlucky

unlucky

13th February FRIDAY!!!

never walk under
a black cat!

unlucky

Yes, Friday the Thirteenth, the
unluckiest day in the year!

First thing this morning, Fishface
came out of the bathroom yelling and
screaming and dripping runny lime-
flavoured jelly everywhere.

I'd filled his Hair Gel jar up with
watered-down jelly so he wouldn't
notice I'd used some (well quite a lot)
for the dog. How was I supposed to
know he'd actually try to use the stuff?

He's had it since Christmas and never
used it before. He must be trying to
impress some girl. Fat chance of that!

26

Today is also the day cousin ('such a sweet girl!') Zoe comes to steal my room and take over my life. No doubt my mum will find her so *sweet* that she'll forget all about her real daughter Carly.

And Dad will become so fond of the useful rent that he'll turn me out of the baby's room next.

The whole house will be rented out to rich people and I will end up in the loft!

me and the rats on my bed of straw in the loft.

I've spent all the evenings this week up in my room with Natalie. Together we've said goodbye to all my favourite things – my notice board, my dressing table with the secret drawer for treasures, the view from my window (I could see all the way to the bus stop which was handy sometimes).

Good bye
to
Carly Ann
Potter's
trusty room

Dad spent all the evenings this week rearranging the baby's room. Mum helped.

Every night, I could hear **BANGS** and **THUMPS** of things being moved and Mum saying, 'Put the bed there. Hmmmmm ... Now try it over there. What about if you move the wardrobe and put it there ... What about if we take that chest out and move the wardrobe and try the bed ... no, put it back the way it was ...'

I put my hands over my ears.

I couldn't bear it.

I was losing my room.

My Space.

My TERRITORY!! ← I looked that one up.

Natalie says I should put it all in my diary because it is a TRAGEDY and we *both* looked up how to spell that.

It is a TRAGEDY and I am a TRAGIC HEROINE.

I am almost homeless.

Natalie says she will buy me an ice lolly or a comic to cheer me up. I say little things like that are not going to make a difference ... but maybe if I had both of them ... and some chocolate ...

There goes the door bell. Stand by for invaders.

ZOE ALERT! ZoE ALERT!

I hate her already.

14th February   Valentine's Day

Wow! Zoe has changed! For one thing she's called Zozo now. For another, her hair is silver. And black. And red. In sort of *stripes*.

'Hi,' she said, cool as cool, and left her mum to do all the talking while she settled into HER (really MY) room. And then this morning … I thought the postman was going to collapse – she had the hugest Valentine card sent to her *plus* four small ones.

Then later in the day someone arrived
with a teddy bear and red heart-shaped
balloons.

And guess what? Fishface got a card
too. So someone out there thinks he's
beautiful. I think whoever she is, she
should have her head examined.

Maybe I should write and tell her
there are plenty more fish in the sea.

And most of them are better looking
than my brother.

I didn't get any cards.

Didn't want any either.

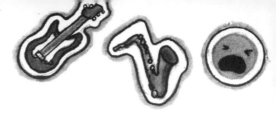

15th February

Settled down for another boring Sunday at home when suddenly the house started shaking. 'It's an earthquake!' said Fishface.

← Fishface diving under the table — coward.

But it was just Zozo's music. She likes to play it loud for what she calls 'the vibe'. No one has the slightest idea what she is talking about and Mum doesn't seem to think she's all that sweet any more.

Hooray!

Perhaps I can have my room back soon!

21st February

Been busy all week so it's taken me till today to get down to the diary. I trust History will forgive me. But I've been a bit tired. I never expected to LIKE sleeping in the baby's room, but I didn't realize how truly HORRIFIC it would be.

It's like sharing a barn with an animal.

All night long it's making snuffling and sucky noises plus squeaks and burps and sounds I probably shouldn't mention in polite society.

SNORE
SNORE
Snuffle
Snuffle
SLURP
BURP
Diagram of Barn Animal Baby sleeping
squeak
POP
POP POP
rattle of toy when kicked by mistake
SUCK SUCK

I never realized how truly RUDE babies are.

And that's not all.

About halfway through every night she wakes up and wails. Then instead of coming to shut her up, Mum has decided to 'leave her time to settle' and I have to tell you THIS DOES NOT WORK.

The worst thing is the baby alarm.

They've got this sort of intercom on the wall so they can hear the baby and talk to her without getting out of their dozy beds. The first night I nearly had a heart attack. I was lying there half asleep trying to ignore the snuffles and wails when the wall spoke!!

YOU SHOULD GO TO SLEEP NOW!! it said.

I closed my eyes like a shot.

Then it started *singing*.

♩ 'Hush a bye baby on the tree top ...' ♫

Of course I realized then it was my mum and the intercom, but it was a bad couple of minutes I'm telling you.

22nd February

Natalie came round but we have nowhere to talk properly now I don't have my room. We tried sitting in my half of the baby's room but it's not the same. Instead of all my pop posters and my signed photo of Girlzone, I've got an alphabet frieze and a Peter Rabbit poster.

Also, I keep banging my head on the baby's mobile of Woodland Folk.

Natalie and me trying to have a proper grown up conversation

I've told Mum that the mouse with the pointy tail will have my eye out one day, but she just tells me not to make a fuss. She says I'll 'soon get used to it', and 'it's only for a few weeks'.

To me it seems like ETERNITY.

I'm getting some good words out of that dictionary!

— PONGT — WHIFF — whiff

WHIFF

PONGT

26th February

Natalie came round tonight and we've had a long talk. Not that it was comfortable, crouched in one half of the baby's room surrounded by the faint whiff of nappy. But I had something important that I really needed to talk to Natalie about.

WHIFF

whiff

Whiff — Whiff

I have SUSPICIONS. It is all about Zoe (or Zozo as she calls herself). On the very rare occasions that she speaks to someone in the house she says, 'I've changed you know. I'm a different person.' That's about ALL she says to Mum.

~~~~~~~~ **EXAMPLE:** ~~~~~~~~

MUM: 'Would you like a cooked breakfast, Zozo?'

(NOTE: When was the last time mum ever asked me if I wanted a cooked breakfast?)

ZOE: 'Naaa ... ta ...'

That's Zozo-speak for "No thank you very much but it was kind of you to offer – especially when you think how long it is since you offered eggs and bacon and suchlike to your own **REAL** child."

MUM: 'But Zozo! You always used to LOVE breakfast. You said my breakfasts were the best you'd ever tasted. Just have a sausage. A little bit of bacon ... '

ZOE: 'Naa ... ta ... I've ... like ... changed. I'm ... different now ...'

At dinner time it was more of the same. 'Have a nice piece of my home-made meat pie, Zoe. You always used to LOVE that.'

'Naaa taaa.'

'Oh dear, Zoe! You seem to be living on fresh air.'

'Well ... see I've changed. I've become a ...'

Then Dad will try his jokes out. It's true his jokes are pathetic but they say that Zoe used to LOVE them.

'What's the weather like up there?' smirks Dad, gazing up at her perched on top of the highest, biggest, silveriest boots you ever saw in your life.

Does Zozo laugh?

She does not.

Does she smile?
Not a bit.

Zoe's mouth

She sort of shrugs as if to say, 'Who IS this sad joker?'

But he doesn't give up easily. He looks at her in her teeny black tunic dress.

'Don't they make skirts to go with those blouses then?' he jokes.

She gives a lopsided grimace which is
supposed to be a smile (I think).

'You've got something growing in your ears!' he tries. She has *enormous* earrings. She looks like she's wearing a pair of particularly large mushrooms.

'Had a bit of a fright have you?' he says. (Today her hair is completely white.)

'Who died?' he asks. (All her clothes are black.) But she just looks as if she doesn't understand the language. As if everyone else is strange and they are all speaking some alien language which she only half understands. And that's when I got my big idea. Oh – but someone's coming. Will write it tomorrow. Must lock this and hide it ASAP*.

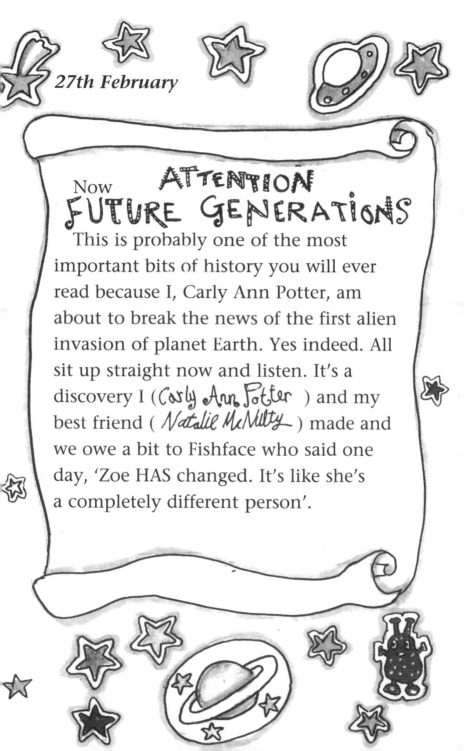

27th February

Now ATTENTION
FUTURE GENERATIONS

This is probably one of the most important bits of history you will ever read because I, Carly Ann Potter, am about to break the news of the first alien invasion of planet Earth. Yes indeed. All sit up straight now and listen. It's a discovery I (*Carly Ann Potter*) and my best friend (*Natalie McNulty*) made and we owe a bit to Fishface who said one day, 'Zoe HAS changed. It's like she's a completely different person'.

'What if …' I said to Natalie. 'What if she IS a completely different person PRETENDING to be Zoe? What if she's disguised as Zoe? What if she's an IMPOSTOR?'

Natalie took it even further. 'What if …' she said. 'What if she isn't even a real PERSON? What if she's … an alien pretending to be Zoe but really she … or HE … or IT is really an alien scout looking at earth to see if the other aliens should come?'

At first I thought this was one of Natalie McNulty's nuttier ideas but the more she explained it, the more possible it seemed. Just look at these photos.

Zoe
before

Zoe
now

1 Zozo is about three times as tall as Zoe ever was.

2 Her legs look like they've been stretched long and thin.

3 Her hair is silver (sometimes). To tell you the truth it's different every day.

4 Natalie says those so-called earrings are probably headphones receiving messages.

5 And those big boots that look like something spacemen wear may really be something spacemen or space*things* wear and the strangest thing of all – and I've saved the spookiest thing till last –

6 Zoe's eyes *were* brown. Now *sometimes* they're brown, I swear they were yellow one day and yesterday – I think – yes, I really do think they were PATTERNED!

Zoe's eyes ← Very → SpOOky!!!

Natalie and I have decided –
we have to get rid of Zoe. First in order
to **SAVE THE WORLD**
and second so that I can
GET MY ROOM BACK

We have made several plans.

1 We could try to find her a job – then
she would move out. BUT who would
employ an alien who hardly says
anything except, 'Naaa taaa'?

2 We could face up to her and tell her
we've found out her secret. We *know*
she is an alien and she'd better move
out quick before we tell Mum and
Dad.

BUT she might not be frightened
of us and might have a death-ray or
similar which would not be nice.

③ Tell Mum and Dad so they can face the death-ray (or similar). **BUT** I don't **WANT** them to face a death-ray and I don't think they'd believe us. I can just see it now.

Me: Mum, we've discovered that Zozo is an alien.
Mum: Probably just a phase she's going through. She's a sweet girl really.
Me: Dad, Zozo is an alien.
Dad: An alien. Hmmm ... still, the rent comes in handy.

What should I do?
The burden of responsibility is o~~rsome~~ or~~gum~~ awesome. I think I'll go round and talk to Natalie again.

1st March   St David's Day

Natalie and I have a plan!!!

We are going to sneak into Zozo's room (MY room) and look for more evidence – clues and suchlike.

Then we're going to have another discussion and work out another plan. We just have to wait for our moment when we can sneak in without fear of being found. Also when we can both do it together because it really is too scary a thing to do all by yourself.

Natalie agrees (actually it was her idea) and together we have written a note so that if something happens to us, the future generations will have some understanding of what went on (and how brave we were). Here's a copy of the note included in this diary as a

HISTORICAL DOCUMENT:

We Carly Ann Potter and Natalie McNulty do hereby inform you that Zozo Perkins (once known as Zoe Perkins) is really an alien (probably). In order to find more evidence for our suspicions we are fearlessly entering her lair (once known as MY room). If we do not come back pledse contact the Police, fire brigade and special FBI departments (as in the X FILES) and let them know so they can continue our brave and good work.

signed Carly Ann Potter (age 10)

Natalie McNulty (10 and a half)

She/IT has gone out!

The weird music has gone off and the front door has slammed. We're going in.

2nd March

I can't bear to write anything.
It was TOO awful.

3rd March

I will never write again.
I am TOO sad.

4th March

Well, just for the sake of future generations who NEED TO KNOW, I will FORCE myself to tell the story, the whole story in all its terrible HORROR and TRAGEDY.

We got into the room.

No trouble.

But once we were in, everything was different.

The first thing we spotted was a huge poster on the wall – a huge poster of the planet Earth.

Natalie McNulty Pointing at Exhibit 11.

Photo by C.A. Potter

'That's a clue!' said Natalie.

Then we saw a strange metal helmet
thing tucked in a corner.

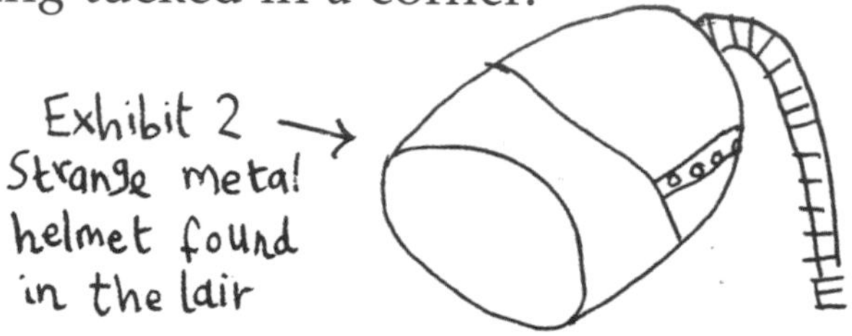

Exhibit 2 →
Strange metal
helmet found
in the lair

'Space helmet!' said Natalie. She
knows about such things – she's
watched millions of space films.

A bit more searching turned up a
book of maps.

'To help her in her invasion,' said
Natalie. And a book called,

The Lonely Planet Guide Book.

'Need I say more?' said Natalie.

And as if that wasn't enough, we
found part of a letter which said:

I haven't told them yet that
I'm really a Vegan.

'That is definite proof!' I said. 'She
admits she's a Vulcan or Martian or
whatever.'

But it was Natalie who found the boxes. Boxes and boxes under the bed – boxes and boxes of things to change your colour. Things to change the colour of your skin, things to change the colour of your hair, AND packets and packets of plastic packs labelled, 'Food Supplements'.

We found all sorts of STRANGE coloured liquids (brown and sludgy green and bright red!!) and pills and extracts.

Exhibit 3. Alien foods

'Obviously alien foods,' said Natalie. But the worst …

On her (what was MY) dressing table
– a small box.

I opened it and found
six bits of eyes staring
up at us: a blue pair,
a dark pair and
a yellow pair – part of
her disguise as a human.

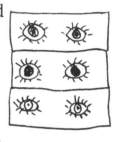

We didn't wait. We ran out of the
room and SCREAMED
for Dad, for Mum, even for Fishface.

5th March

I had to stop at that point of the story.
It was a lot to write. My hand was
getting ecshorsted exhauste really tired
and I was getting a hard lump on my
finger from the agony of such intense
writing.

Also, the next bit of the story is really horrible. I don't even want to think about it, let alone WRITE about it.

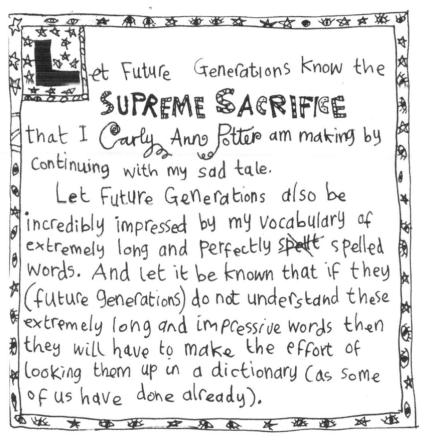

Let Future Generations know the

SUPREME SACRIFICE

that I Carly Anno Potter am making by continuing with my sad tale.

Let Future Generations also be incredibly impressed by my vocabulary of extremely long and perfectly spelt spelled words. And let it be known that if they (future generations) do not understand these extremely long and impressive words then they will have to make the effort of looking them up in a dictionary (as some of us have done already).

Oh – I've run out of time for writing this. Got to go. Will continue tomorrow (solemn promise).

6th March

So … there I was at the top of the stairs screaming:

And there was Dad bounding up the stairs saying, 'What is it … what? What?'

And there was Mum following saying, 'Sh! The baby. You'll wake the baby.'

And there was Fishface saying, 'If you call me Fishface once more I swear I'll …'

And (oh, oh, oh,) there was ZOZO – behind them.

Yes, there she was on her high silver boots with her mushroom earrings, her black tunic, her silver hair and her GREEN AND SILVER EYES!

And she was clutching a gun (or death ray or similar) and pointing it at us.

I screamed: AAAGGAHH!!

And then I fell into merciful unconsciousness (which is easier to do than it is to spell – and just means I fainted).

Well actually, I fell over. But we writers and figures of historical importance are allowed to e~~ggag~~ exaggerate.

You should see the size of the writing lump on my finger now. It is AGONY writing this. I will have to seek emergency treatment.

oops →

a bit too much
emergency treatment
~~ointment~~

7th March

'We're all going to die!'

'She's invading the planet!'

'Look out! She's got a gun (or death-ray or similar)!' I shouted.

But Fishface just said: 'Gun!! That's a hairdryer, you twit. She's been doing my hair.'

And then I got my first good look at Fishface.

Fishface →
hair all silver
and spiky !!

'Oh, AARRGGH! They've got Fishface! He's become one of them!' I cried.

Fishface just laughed.

Dad blinked and scratched his head.

And what did Mum say to this WORLD THREATENING news? She said, 'You HAVE woken the baby up now. Honestly!'

Zozo was smiling her crooked weird smile and blinking her green and silver eyes.

Bit by bit it all came out.

'Look at her silver space boots!' I cried.

'What would YOU know about fashion?' sniggered Fishface.

'Look at all these posters of planets ...'

'Mmm,' said Dad. 'Zoe's just been telling us all about her concern for the planet. She's been explaining that all this time she's really been a vegan ...'

'There, there! You see! She admits she's a ...'

'Vegan,' said Fishface, very slowly as if talking to an idiot. 'A vegan is a sort of vegetarian – doesn't eat meat or animal products. What did you think a vegan was – someone who comes from the planet Vegas? Ha!'

Then he collapsed in giggles.

Natalie had gone very quiet.

But I wasn't going to give up.

'What about her eyes then – Look! Green and SILVER eyes. How do you explain *that* away? Ha!'

8th March

Well, I'd never heard of coloured contact lenses. Sounds a weird idea to me. I mean why would anybody WANT to change their eye colour, whatever the fashion mags say? Anyway, that's what they were. She even took one out (yerk!) to show me. She just put her hand to her eye and popped out the silver lens leaving herself with only one silver and green alien-looking lens, and one very normal-looking brown eye blinking at me.

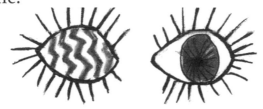

I expect you've figured the rest out. The colour-change things were (yes, you've guessed) make-up.

The maps and guide books were just ... maps and guide books.

The food supplements and pills were vitamins and stuff because she could hardly eat any of our non-vegan food.

And the helmet thing? That was an attachment to the famous hairdryer that really DID look like a death-ray (or similar).

I felt so STUPID.

Fishface disguised as hedgehog →

Hairdryer disguised as Death Ray

And of course my ever-loving family are now always laughing and teasing me. They will never let me forget it.

For instance: when the phone rings and it's Natalie for me, my dad says, 'Mission control needs urgent communication'. Ha ha.

When Fishface is supposed to be calling me down to eat (and believe me I have no wish ever to eat again), he shouts, 'Beam yourself down, Spotty!'

Even Mum spraying round the
kitchen with her Mr Gleam spray can't
resist aiming it at me and giggling,

Ha, ha, ha. Very funny I DON'T think.
Fishface has taken to offering me bits
of chocolate (not like him to be so
generous). He only does it so he can get
a few more cruel jibes in. Example:

'Anyone for a chunk of this Galaxy –
while there's some left!'

'Or maybe a little bit of MARS?'

'Or why not just go for the whole
Milky Way!'*

I will never live down the shame.

*Note for Future Generations: for some reason
lots of chocolate bars are called after planets.
(I don't know why – maybe they're supposed
to taste out of this world.)

14th March

Natalie came round and Zoe and Fishface suggested we all went out to Laser Quest.*

I said I would rather DIE than go through the humiliation of any more space teasing – but Natalie said she'd heard it was really cool, and after all *they* were paying, so why not go?

So we did.

I *had* to go, out of friendship to Natalie. And, out of friendship to Natalie, I joined in – and, hey, I WON!!

Natalie and I are thinking of going again. But not with Zozo. She's moving out next week. She found a job.

So it looks like I've got my room back after all, which is **excellent**.

---

* Future Generations should know this is a big dark place where you pay to run around with a backpack and a pretend space gun, zapping each other to get points.

I'm very happy about that. But *in a way* I will miss Zozo. I learnt a lot from knowing her and am now a much wiser, calmer, and more understanding person – not so likely to LEAP to ideas – or at least not so likely to tell my brother about them.

I've learned understanding, tolerance, and how to put silver streaks in my hair.

Now what am I going to do for new adventures without an alien invasion to worry about? I suppose I could take up roller blading, or jogging, or maybe mountaineering or skydiving. Yes! Skydiving would be good.

But for the moment I think I'll just go round and talk to Natalie.

About the author

I've written more than
50 books for children,
but this is the first time
I've written in the form
of a diary. Of course,
I've often tried to write
a diary of my own –
but I've never managed to
get beyond the 15th January. It was fun
getting under the skin of a character like
Carly Ann Potter – imagining what she
would think, what she would say and
how she would say it.